A LEARNING CHURCH

CALLED TO NEW LIFE

Companion book:

Investors in People in the Church:
The Introduction of the Investors Standard in Dioceses,
Parishes and Cathedrals,
A report of a Board of Education Task Group
by Julian Cummins and Ian Stubbs
(Church House Publishing, 1999)

GS Misc 546

CALLED TO NEW LIFE

The World of Lay Discipleship

A report prepared
by a Working Group
of the Board of Education

CHURCH HOUSE
PUBLISHING

Church House Publishing
Church House
Great Smith Street
London
SW1P 3NZ

ISBN 0 7151 4923 7

Published 1999 for the Board of Education of the Church of England by
Church House Publishing

**This report has only the authority of the Working Group which produced it;
it has been approved by the Board of Education.**

Printed by The Cromwell Press Ltd, Trowbridge, Wiltshire

Contents

Members of the Working Group

The following people served as members of the Working Group:

Mr Peter Middlemiss

Chairman of the Group
Warden of Holland House; member
of General Synod, the Board of Education
and the Voluntary and Continuing
Education Committee

Miss Sheila Addison

Adult Education and Training Officer,
Diocese of Peterborough

Miss Isabel Booth Clibborn

Children's Work Adviser, Diocese
of Manchester

Professor Walter James

Board of Education and Voluntary
and Continuing Education Committee
member

Dr Gareth Jones

Theological Consultant to the House
of Bishops and Theological Secretary
to the Council for Christian Unity

Ms Maggie Pickup

Director of St Peter's Saltley Trust

Mrs Hilary Ineson

Secretary to the Group
Adviser in Adult Education and Training,
Board of Education

Remit of the Working Group

1.   To evaluate what has happened since the publication of *All Are Called* and *Called to Be Adult Disciples*.

     a)   To follow up previous work – to examine and evaluate the theology, practice and action taken in dioceses.

     b)   To examine and clarify the difficulties the Church has experienced in effectively supporting the discipleship of lay people.

2.   To look at the role and needs of laity in the Church of the twenty-first century in mission, service and discipleship, to develop strategies to enable the Church to support and value the work of lay Christians in their daily lives.

One of the recommendations in *Called to Be Adult Disciples* was that Synod should ensure that Working Groups should contain a good proportion of lay representation. This Working Group was a totally lay group.

Foreword

As we move towards the third millennium, Jesus continues to call his disciples to 'Follow me'. It is a call to faithful Christian living in a world that often seems hostile, alien or just apathetic, and where challenges to such a way of life change with increasing rapidity. Yet it is a world in which people are asking searching and profound questions.

Over the last twenty years lay people have taken an increasing role in the life of the local church. Diocesan provision for their training and education has increased and many lay people are now theologically educated in a way they have never been before.

This report focuses on those lay people whose main area of discipleship living is in their daily lives of work, leisure, family and voluntary action. It begins with the stories of six such lay people and these stories form the basis for thinking about how successful the Church is at enabling lay people to take seriously this discipleship living.

The report shows the strengths and weaknesses of the Church in its attempts to enable lay people to increase their confidence in their faith understanding and to put it into action. From the basis of their inquiry into what has happened since the publication of *All Are Called* (1985) and *Called to be Adult Disciples* (1987), the Working Group have developed their theological understanding of the demands on lay people and suggest some strategies for future developments.

I commend this report to you.

✠ Stephen Venner

Bishop of Middleton, Chair of the Voluntary and Continuing Education Committee of the Board of Education

Acknowledgements

The Working Group would like to thank all those people who responded to requests for information and comment, particularly diocesan officers for adult education and lay training, Industrial Missioners, the Iona Community, members of General Synod, young adults in dioceses and members of Christians in Public Life.

Introduction

The new millennium is being heralded as a 'hinge of history', a time for review of what has gone before and a unique opportunity to think afresh about many of our most basic assumptions. We are being encouraged to seize this chance to reflect on what is important to us and to look at new ways of affirming our belief and values. One of the key areas for such reflection is that of lay discipleship, a subject that has received extensive previous consideration.

In 1983 the General Synod's Board of Education set up a Working Party to look at the theology of the laity. Its conclusions were published in 1985 as *All Are Called*.[1] General Synod debated a follow-up report *Called to Be Adult Disciples*[2] in 1987. Both reports called on the Church to value and affirm the discipleship of all lay people, and especially those whose call was specifically focused on their everyday life of work, home and leisure. Together they made recommendations about how the Church could offer resources to help such laity fulfil that calling.

A number of other churches also produced reports at that time, illustrating a degree of ecumenical convergence on the nature of the vocation of every Christian. For example, the Roman Catholic Church's *Christifideles Laici*,[3] published in 1989, provided a theological basis for understanding the nature of the baptismal call. Similarly, the Methodist Church's *The Ministry of the Whole People of God* (1988)[4] saw the affirmation of the ministry of the whole *laos* as fundamental to the life of the Church. Both documents, alongside the work of other churches, emphasized the significance of lay discipleship both in the Church and in the world.

The scope of this report is to consider lay discipleship in today's world, in the process building upon the work done in the 1980s. We have examined some ways in which lay discipleship has been supported by the work done since the 1980s in various dioceses of the Church of England. What we have then attempted to do is identify those themes and theological questions that seem to arise naturally from the situations we have encountered. In this way our reflection has been guided by the particular lived experiences of lay Christians as they witness to their faith in the contemporary world.

It follows, consequently, that we have not attempted to provide a general theology of what it is to be a Christian today. Such guidance has been provided elsewhere and can be seen in very simple form, for example in 'A Short Guide to the Duties of Church Membership for Members of the Church of England', written by the Archbishops of Canterbury and York. Nor have we engaged with many of the complex ecclesiological questions that are rightly regarded as also significant to the continuing life of the Church. Instead, we have concentrated upon the specific challenges of lay discipleship, addressing issues of empowerment and responsibility as they pertain to the work of the people of God.

What the reader will find in the following pages, therefore, is a focus upon the laity, by which we mean those members of the Body of Christ who are called not to be ordained. Starting with a consideration of six scenarios and stories coming from the Diocese of Peterborough, the report moves from such particular experiences to an elaboration of the findings of further case studies. It then offers some theological reflections upon this material, and upon possible strategies for supporting lay disciples.

1

The Things they Say and the Stories they Tell in the Diocese of Peterborough

Introduction

Within this chapter there are several stories that are told in order to set the scene and establish our findings in a contemporary context:

- the story of a diocesan initiative and its development;

- the picture presented by six scenarios drawn from a survey of the views of 200 lay Christians from various age groups and walks of life;

- six personal stories, illustrative of the common themes that emerged, that seem to beg further questions and call for some response by the Church locally and nationally.

These illustrations from one particular diocese emphasize the diverse challenges facing lay disciples.

The story of a diocesan initiative

At the beginning of the Decade of Evangelism a group of Christian businessmen in the Diocese of Peterborough produced a report about the issues and difficulties that they and others experienced when trying to live out their faith at work. This was in response to a request to do so from the bishop, who was also concerned to review Industrial Mission and discern the directions that this ministry might take in the 1990s. Many in the diocese remember that Bishop Bill Westwood frequently reminded people that the Scriptures record Jesus as saying 'God so loved the WORLD that he gave his only Son' and not 'God so loved the CHURCH'. He was concerned that all who are called to serve God in their places of employment should feel affirmed and helped to see that work is a worthy calling. It was his view that this perception should be reflected in the practice of the Church, as well as be recognized as the way of God.

The story that emerged as a result of the investigations done by this group had the following features:

- In 1991 the Diocesan Synod set up the 'People and Work Programme', a lay-led project to complement the work of the two Industrial Chaplains. The diocese initially funded this with a small budget for administrative costs and to produce resources to help groups.

- The Diocesan Guild of Centurions together with the Church Army then made it possible to fund a full-time director of the programme during the second phase.

- Consideration is now being given to ways in which this work may be more fully integrated into the whole adult education and training work of the diocese.

- A co-ordinating committee has been set up to include a wider representation than just businessmen.

- A lay-led programme of group activities across the diocese was developed in which people were able to meet for 'one-off' or a continuous series of discussions, teaching or action according to the needs of the people in the group. One group looked at ways in which the Church might draw attention to the knock-on effects of late payment of invoices, another set up a support group for those recently made redundant, a third considered ways in which they could provide advice and resources for job seekers.

- The groups are generally supported by a member of the Co-ordinating Committee, though not necessarily led by them.

- Industrial Chaplains, the Diocesan Officer for Continuing Ministerial Education and the Diocesan Lay Training Officer served as a resource to the programme.

The overall aim of the People and Work Programme is 'to encourage and equip Christians living out their faith in the workplace'. The key objectives are:

- to work in partnership with local churches, calling on the support and theological expertise of the ordained ministry and offering resources and advice on how the gaps between church worship and teaching and the worlds of work may be bridged;

- to set up and resource local groups across the diocese in order to give Christians of all denominations the chance to meet regularly to discuss questions of faith and work;

- to provide training opportunities and materials for both individual and group study;

- to organize conferences and study days which examine issues faced by Christians at work;

- to liaise with similar projects in other parts of the country.

The People and Work Programme exists mainly to support those who are in paid employment, full time or part time, but also recognizes the needs of those who work in voluntary service in the community or within the home.

In order to be able to submit evidence for this report, a broad brush survey was carried out within the same diocese to gain something of the picture a decade on. The questionnaire was not limited to people at work but also included life in the family, the community, in places of leisure and in political and social life. The process was simple:

- A questionnaire was devised and given to 200 lay Christians from various walks of life, church traditions, environments and age groups.

- From the 200 replies, 20 people were invited to develop the story that they had begun to write as part of the questionnaire.

- These stories were analysed and set against the more general picture that emerged from the responses of the other 180. From this analysis, six scenarios emerged. They are not surprising, but may serve to illustrate the fuller story in this report.

The scenarios

1. People who feel that the Church does not, and could not, understand the issues they face from Monday to Saturday.

2. People who want to escape their Monday to Saturday lives and want the Church to be a haven for Sunday that does not remind them of the pressures and difficulties they face during the week.

3. People who see the Church as their real work and paid employment in some other organization as the means by which they can afford to do it.

4.   People who long for support and help in identifying a Christian perspective on issues that arise in their lives.

5.   People who lack the confidence to be adult disciples because the Church seems to tell them that they have to be accredited before they may speak of their faith or raise questions that may lead to moral and ethical debate.

6.   People who feel that the Church has much to say about what is perceived as the 'softer places of work', e.g. service industries, work at home . . . as opposed to the 'tougher world' of business, commerce, manufacturing industry . . .

The stories

1.   Those who feel that the Church does not or could not understand the issues they face from Monday to Saturday.

The issues include:

● management of time within the context of the range of God-given responsibilities: family, work, community contribution, church and rest/relaxation;

● balance of life between the desire to engage in activities that extend the kingdom of God and the desire to pursue interests that may simply be enjoyable for their own sake;

● concerns about how money should be accrued in the first place and then used 'Christianly';

● the expectation that in the workplace, in community, political and civic life, people should be 'thrusting', assertive if not aggressive, demanding and to some extent manipulative – qualities which seem to run counter to the teaching of the Church;

● frustration that, while pious platitudes from the Church about justice, peace, forgiveness . . . may raise the questions, there is little to help people to deal with the hard realities of injustice, conflict and a desire for retribution in much of life, especially in the workplace;

● difficulties in dealing with values that are relative when the Church tends to be concerned with absolutes;

- embarrassment with a lifestyle outside the Church that is daily concerned with performance measures, outcomes and value-added concepts when the Church speaks of 'letting go and letting God'.

These issues are representative of many which people felt could not be understood by the Church and certainly were seldom addressed within the teaching of the Church.

It seems that the overriding emotion felt by these people was not so much frustration at the lack of understanding by the Church but guilt that they were leading lives that seemed to be in conflict with their understanding of the gospel. There was also frustration expressed about the failure of the Church to provide a forum where they could explore these issues and try to deal with them.

Some said that they felt that they had to go outside the local congregation to get this support: deanery or diocesan groups or just gatherings of like-minded people. Others were unaware that this was possible. Some thought it might be a disloyal thing to do because, by implication, they would be criticizing their local church. Perhaps those who feel that they may need a different forum are beginning to answer their own questions in that the local church congregation may not necessarily be the best place to grapple with these issues.

Margaret's story

I work in a café in a small market town which receives several tourists, especially at the weekends. I work part-time but when things are really busy I frequently find myself working a full week. I work all day on Saturdays. The work is very tiring and sometimes very frustrating but there are many opportunities to relate to people; some are regulars who come in for a cup of tea and stay for two or three hours, some are Saturday shoppers wanting refreshment and a rest, some are passers-by who want the best service and in a hurry and almost all want to talk about their lives. I love to listen to their stories: about their journeys, their elderly parents who take a lot of their time, their work and their love lives. It seems that people will talk to a comparative stranger like me about all manner of personal matters. When I go to church on Sunday I find that prayers, sermon illustrations and visiting speakers all seem to focus on 'important' jobs such as being a teacher, a doctor, a policeman or a parent. I am none of these and I gain the impression that the vicar and others think that I am in a *little job for 'pin money' but that it doesn't have much significance or contribute much to anything. As a result I don't find anything within the worship that speaks to me about my life through the week, so I depend on my personal prayer to help me to serve God in my work. When I was asked to think about this I came to realize that I cannot expect people to understand what I do in my work and that the church is not the place to help me in that aspect of my life.*

2. Those who want to escape from their Monday to Saturday lives and want the church to be a haven for Sunday that does not remind them of the pressures and difficulties they face during the week.

These people come at the matter with a very different perspective from those represented in Scenario 1. Their comments and reflections give rise to the following:

- To some extent these people see Sunday worship as a separate activity in their lives, rather like joining a hobby group. You participate for the period of the gathering with like-minded friends but for the rest of your life your faith may only have a passive connection. The person you are reflects your faith but the issues and beliefs are for private thought or conversation with only those who are also in the 'holy club'.

- People do not think it is appropriate to mix the 'things of God' with the rather dirty world of commerce or industry or politics or with the culture of ambition or status. God is above such matters and it is embarrassing to say the least to suggest that he might become implicated beyond prayer in which we ask him to help us to bear the exigencies of the week.

- Some feel it to be an admission of spiritual failure to reveal that the world of the weekday was rather difficult. They did not feel confident enough, or there were more appropriate places in which to discuss the harsh realities of life outside the cosy atmosphere of Sunday worship. This attitude applied as much to those struggling with recalcitrant teenage children as to people with senior responsibilities in the workplace. They feel that worship is a time to forget these matters and that life will go on and that the teaching and the sacraments will sustain them without the need for reminders of the rigours of life 'outside'.

- Others feel that as they have to live with so much change in their everyday lives, they hope that the Church will be more consistent and not change so that they may have some connections with the past. There were several references to the God 'who is the same yesterday and for ever' in support of their view that the way the Church can best offer support is to remain constant and still be the haven they have come to rely on.

Jeremy's story

I work as a senior salesman in a reputable car showroom. Much of the time at work is spent walking around the showroom trying to engage people who are 'just looking'. We are on commission so there is quite a lot of pressure to make a sale. I am not proud of some of the things I find myself saying in order to get people to become interested in a particular car. The problem is that it is not until I think about it afterwards that I wonder if a Christian should exaggerate or use psychological pressure such as flattery to make profit. These matters are not discussed in our team meetings at work. On a few occasions I have tried to open up the subject with our Unit Manager because there are others who are not Christians but who worry about the morality of some of the training we are given.

As far as church is concerned I find that I am too embarrassed to discuss these things. Most people I meet at church seem very 'together'. I can't imagine them being involved in some of the things we have to do when selling cars. I belong to a house group but mostly we talk about the children and schools and relationships, etc. In any case I don't really want to talk about work when I am off duty, especially on Sundays. I want to forget about it all until Monday morning.

3. Those who see the Church as their real work and paid employment in some other organization as the means by which they can afford to do it.

This was a common view in the sample. The following issues emerged:

- People seemed to want to serve God but had a limited concept of how they might do this outside the institution of the Church.

- They had been led to believe that service within the institution of the Church was a higher calling than service in the world.

- They felt that as there were few opportunities for paid employment within the Church they had to become 'tent-makers' to be solvent while leaving sufficient time and energy for the 'real work' to be done in the Church.

- Almost every person in this category admitted that they had little commitment to the company for which they work and that work was simply a means to an end.

- When challenged about the ethical issues that surround this area all said it would be different if they were in management but as members of a basic workforce they saw some biblical evidence for this view of service to God.

Steve's story

When I was asked to tell my story about how my faith and my work related I was puzzled. I believe that my main calling is to serve God and that means that I should make sure that I organize my life in such a way that I can give him the most and the best. I am well qualified and have quite a lot of experience as a TV engineer. I have had several offers of courses that would lead to promotion and therefore a better salary. Since I became a Christian five years ago I have turned down these offers because I realize that more responsibility means longer hours and that would take me more away from serving God. People at work just don't understand this and think that I am rather odd. However, I think that all my spare time should be spent with Christians and working in the church. I don't talk about my work at church as a rule because it doesn't seem relevant. Church and the world are separate. Unfortunately, we have to earn a living and for me that is the only valid reason for going to work. I have to be a 'tent-maker' in order to help to build a 'Temple'. In the long run the church benefits because earners can be givers. Occasionally, I am asked to mend the TVs of people in the church and I am glad to do that as part of my Christian service, otherwise there is no real connection between my life at work for 38 hours a week and my work in the church for around 25 hours a week.

4. Those who long for support and help in identifying a Christian perspective on issues that arise in their lives.

Many of the people in the sample were those currently attending a diocesan course. All said that they might have had a different view prior to attending the course. In this sense their responses may not be typical. However, there were many in this category and all those on the course who completed the questionnaire expressed this view. The implications might be very far reaching but the following points emerged:

- People felt inadequate when discussing ethical and moral issues with people who would not call themselves Christians. They expressed the view that there never seemed to be time within the life of the local church to discuss questions such as debt (personal and world), financial management, life (abortion, euthanasia), use of leisure and time, cloning and other issues concerned with genetic engineering.

- People wanted more opportunity for personal pastoral care from within the Church in which they had time to examine their own position about a number of issues concerned with an outworking of their faith, e.g. issues related to justice, peace and economy. Most said that the clergy were overpressed and not in a position to give time to this, yet seemed to be anxious about groups gathering to discuss such matters without them.

- Some were critical of the low level of expectation when discussion groups were formed in the local church. Such groups seemed to depend on basic Bible exposition and not to take people on from that to interpretation for the present generation locally or globally.

- Some had been given books to read which had been helpful but which made the need for challenging discussion even more pertinent.

● The issue that emerged most forcefully was that people were meeting others in their families, at work, in pubs and clubs, within their neighbourhood who expected that Christians might have a different perspective and that they were interested in what the Church has to say about . . .

Ruth's story

Don't get me wrong, I love Bible study and learning about all the background information that brings the Bible to life. When our rector does it he is brilliant, but he never relates it to everyday life today. He always says that we must interpret it for ourselves. Well I need some help with that. I work as a receptionist in a medical centre. Both on the phone and in person, people ask me the most bizarre questions. I am quite 'up front' about being a Christian and almost everyone knows that I am very active in the church. As many of the people who come to the centre are anxious and sometimes very distressed, I am the first person they meet and part of my job is to provide care and support as well as make appointments. People ask me really deep questions about faith and life and although I have been going to church for about 35 years I am often at a loss to answer them. People ask about things like abortion and euthanasia and faith healing and what God thinks about these things. A lot of these people never darken the door of a church except perhaps at Christmas, so I know that whatever I say may be the only conversation about God they may ever have. Can I get my church to discuss these really knotty questions? No! I get promises that one day we will or I'm told 'You can't go round upsetting people by raising such controversial issues.'

5. Those who lack the confidence to be adult disciples because the Church seems to tell them that they have to be accredited before they may speak of their faith or raise questions that may lead to spiritual, moral or ethical debate.

Within the sample there seemed to be a growing awareness that all are called to speak of the God whom they worship and the faith they have and to tell their story. However, despite a growing recognition of this there were many who felt that they lacked the confidence because there are those who have been specially trained to explain the faith. Some issues that people thought should be addressed are:

- In order to be adult disciples do we all have to be able to speak of our faith? Are we less than adequate if we fail to take the opportunities to do so?

- People feel that what they have to say lacks any currency unless they have some accreditation from the Church which gives them permission to speak or engage in theological debate.

- People feel that the leaders of the Church become edgy when they want to speak of matters that have a deeper theological significance than the average Christian may have experienced. Readers were among those said most jealously to protect their status and to question the right of 'unauthorized' speakers. This attitude within the Church was said to reduce the confidence of people serving God in the world and being asked questions along the way.

Simon's story

I'd love to have the opportunity to speak at the morning service at our church. We have a congregation of about 75 people and they come from across the age groups and from different walks of life. I am in my thirties and work in a paper distribution company, in middle management. I love my work and am regarded as quite successful in that I have had early promotions along the way since leaving university. I work very hard and apart from my family, work takes up most of my life, either on the job or in thinking time. I don't see work as a drudgery, my colleagues are good friends and, although the pressure is always on to make the year's profits exceed those of the previous year, we manage to do this within an ethical framework which is well understood. The company is a 'workers' co-operative' which means that not only do we share the profits, but we share the responsibility and the feeling of ownership. I feel that there is so much that I learn from my work that could relate to the worship and teaching in the church. I put this idea to the PCC and several people were really enthusiastic about it. The vicar said he would take the idea to the Ministry Team. Almost a year went by and I heard nothing, so I asked the vicar about it. He said that it had been discussed but the team members, especially the readers, were not happy about someone who had not studied theology preaching in the main service on a

Sunday. He said that he thought I might speak at a house group meeting. He then asked me if I considered whether God was calling me to be a reader! I was very disappointed. The readers in our church are lovely people but they are all retired so perhaps they find it difficult to remember the joys and sorrows of being a Christian in a busy workplace. It seems a pity that we can't share our experience with fellow Christians without having a licence from the bishop to do so.

6. Those who feel that the Church has much to say about what is perceived as the 'softer places of work', e.g. service industries, work at home . . . as opposed to the 'tougher world' of business, commerce, manufacturing industry . . .

Many people in the survey thought that the Church tried hard to root the teaching and the intercessory life of the Church in the world from which they thought people came. However, the following points emerged:

- Examples in sermons and the focus of much of the prayer concerned family life, education, health service and emergency services rather than those who work in retail, manufacturing, financial services, management of profit-making organizations.

- 'Professional' work seemed to be highlighted more than that of those who are artisans, shop-floor workers, etc.

- Examples of women's discipleship seemed to suggest that all were in the home or worked as employees and 'workers' rather than in management.

- Most of the Church's visiting programmes and mission work focus on homes, residential care homes, schools and hospitals and few visits, approaches or invitations are made to factories, garages, retail outlets, farms, offices, etc. unless there is a plea for funds or sponsorship.

- People made the point that if their lives were bound up in some of these more commercial environments they felt even more in need of the Church's support and affirmation.

Pam's story

I am a chartered accountant and one of the difficulties for me is to battle against the culture which suggests that accountants run the country, are 'hard-nosed' and mostly lacking in the ability to see the human being behind a client. As a woman and a Christian I have added complications in the environment in which I work. I could cope with all this if I found some real understanding about the issues I face when I am involved in my church.

I am also a parent so I appreciate some of the ways in which that role is affirmed and prayed for. People speak caringly about the pressures of having to travel to the City every day on trains that are often late. However, if I start to talk about the issues that are specific to being an accountant there seem to be embarrassment and jokes from the treasurer about when I am ready to take over from him. The last thing I want to do is handle more money. However, I would like to get together with others who face similar issues. I once suggested this to our curate and she said that most clergy feel the need to stay within those areas they understand and that it is difficult to ask leaders to put themselves into a position where they may not have the answers.

I don't need them to help me be an accountant; I need someone to help me think about the biblical/theological perspectives on a life which is bound up with law and the management of other people's resources. I don't believe that I should have gained so much experience and insight and then have no space to reflect on this with others within the totality of my life. Perhaps this is too much to expect of my own church and instead I should be setting up a support group of like-minded people. There is definitely a need as far as I can see.

Conclusion

This survey, based on a questionnaire and written and spoken stories, reveals that although the Church tries to relate to the lives of the people who form that Church there are many areas of life that seem to be ignored.

Within the liturgy of the Eucharist people are invited to pray these words: 'Send us out in the power of your Spirit to live and work to your praise and glory.' Many people are well aware that God is concerned for every aspect of our lives and that his Spirit is already there ahead of them wherever they go. However, the survey gives a clear message that the Church, i.e. the whole 'Body of Christ', categorizes and stereotypes and places a 'value-added' perspective on some of the places to which God calls us to serve him. This seems to diminish the discipleship of many people who believe that they are called to serve him in the world.

2

The Context

The issues and stories from people living and worshipping in one diocese described in Chapter 1 raise questions that it is important to consider. Many of the people who contributed evidence to the Peterborough survey said or implied that they feel themselves to be 'lay' because they regard themselves as theologically untutored and amateur, especially when called to speak of their faith. They have taken on the dictionary definition of the word 'lay', i.e. 'unprofessional; amateur' (*Collins English Dictionary*).

In a society in which qualifications and accreditation are highly prized, many people in the Church seem to have accepted the dictum that unless you have the appropriate experience and have followed specific courses of study you should regard yourself as 'lay'. Many meet this notion when dealing with the health service, the teaching profession, the law . . .

The stories you have read, however, reveal people who bring a great deal of experience combined with an ability to reflect theologically upon it. A key issue for the Church is to give such people the confidence to see that they have a specific calling to serve God in the world and to accept that they have a priestly ministry because they are willing to offer themselves to God by serving in his world.

Who are the laity?

We take as our basis for this work the belief that the Church is the whole people, the Body of Christ in the world. We are the Church through our baptism, and baptism is the primary call. The 'whole people' is called to mission and ministry, to worship God and serve the world Jesus died to save. Within the people there are distinctive and diverse calls. Some are called to ordination as deacons, priests and bishops; most are called to lay discipleship. This report is concerned with those called to the lay life, to whom we will refer as the laity or lay people. Our focus of concern is even more specific. Some of the laity are also called to take on a role in the local church – as part of a local ministry team, as a lay leader involved in collaborative ministry, as a Sunday School teacher or Bible study group leader. That more specific part of their call to discipleship has not been part of our brief: our focus is on the call to lay people to live out their faith in their daily (and what is sometimes called secular) lives.

We have struggled not to differentiate between Church and world, though sometimes in order to make a point we may have fallen into that trap. We have also tried hard not to put barriers between the call to the lay life and the call to ordination. All Christians are called to discipleship in daily life, whether ordained or not. We want to highlight those lay people whose vocation is often undervalued simply because it is exercised as the Church dispersed through the fabric of work, family and community and is therefore more difficult to identify and quantify.

Although our focus is on adult laity we recognize that much of what we say in this document also applies to children and young people as they live out their lives as the Church through their everyday experience. Many of them would recognize the experience of the adults described here.

One advantage of starting with an analysis of a particular situation in a specific diocese (Peterborough) is that it makes us think not of 'lay discipleship' the concept, but rather of flesh-and-blood individuals who are lay disciples. We see that lay disciples bring to the Church a very great diversity of talents, convictions, professions, attitudes, pastimes and responsibilities. Often, too, they bring with them pain and sorrow, rejection and isolation. All of these, good and bad, are memories that shape and focus their faith and their lives. To recognize this is to recognize the reality of lay discipleship.

At the same time, however, it is also necessary to affirm that today's generations of lay disciples are not alone: they follow (and precede) other generations, with whom they share a common Christian identity. There is a need, consequently, to speak generally of the laity, even if we are always mindful of the *palpable* character of individuals and their communities. This is an argument recently expressed in Resolution 111.22 from the 1998 Lambeth Conference of the Bishops of the Anglican Communion. This resolution is worth quoting in full precisely because it represents the common agreement of bishops drawn from a wide diversity of provinces:

15

> This Conference:
>
> - *affirms our trust in the power of God's Spirit to ensure that all persons are made full disciples and equally members of the Body of Christ and the people or laos of God by their baptism;*
>
> - *while recognising the necessity of ordained ministry and special responsibilities which are given to various members of the Body, also recognises that all the baptised share in the common priesthood of the Churches that the life, practice, polity and liturgy of churches everywhere should exemplify this understanding of our community and common life, and;*
>
> - *affirms that in baptism all are called to personal commitment to Jesus Christ and should be given education and opportunity for ministries which include worship, witness, service and acts of forgiveness and reconciliation in the setting of their daily life and work.*

The juxtaposition of Peterborough and Lambeth is helpful because it tells us something important about the creative tension that exists within any treatment of lay discipleship. On the one hand, lay disciples are always women and men, children and adults, people with names and faces and stories who demand our attention; for listening to their voices is often the best way to hear our own. On the other hand, lay disciples are members of the one Body of Christ, which Body remains eternally God's revelation to the world. The paradox confronting us when we want to talk about lay disciples, consequently, is that one God speaks to us in many different ways, through many different people. Recognizing that human diversity is empowered by divine unity is one of the most important ways in which we can understand our relationship with God and with each other.

The world context

The stories told in Chapter 1 reveal that the world in which people live, move and have their being is radically changed from that in which their predecessors lived. It is a world in which work is challenging and satisfying for some of those who have it, but not for everyone. In an increasingly competitive milieu, work subjects growing numbers to the relentless pressures of meeting sales targets and adopting questionable practices. The world of work is more insecure and those who are in work are working longer hours and more intensively, whilst others have no work at all.[1] The expectations of the world of work and those of their Christian faith are situations of conflict for many lay people. Some feel that the only way to survive is to keep the two areas of life in separate boxes.

It is also a world characterized by rapid change; traditional modes of thinking and acting will be more readily perceived as no longer relevant. In a time of change and diversity, Christians encounter people who do not share their faith. Such people may look to them in secular and informal situations to illuminate aspects of Christian belief – something which they may feel ill equipped to do.

The family life people experience is no longer uniform. The relationships and status of each member within the family are no longer settled. Ethical issues are now more widely encountered. Today, abortion is one of the more prominent in a range of widespread concerns which previously only a few had to consider.

Technological change has invested power in human beings which gives them more responsibility for the maintenance of the environment and at the same time invests them with more capacity to degrade or destroy it. The extension of choice to areas of life which were previously constrained by tradition or submission to circumstances has increased personal encounters with questions of value and belief. The Internet and World Wide Web, homes in which a computer is commonplace, digital television and the expansion of technology will all mean even more rapid change in the next few years. By 2008 all television will be digital, giving access to such technology to every home with a TV. The generation that is at school at present will be computer literate in the way that older generations were able to read and write. For them the technology will be an everyday part of life.

Extensive though change has been, it will accelerate and be even more pervasive during the twenty-first century. The need for learning throughout the lifespan to become a reality and not merely an aspiration will be critical if people are to make sense of their lives and make choices that are life enhancing. Lifelong learning, a major part of Government policy, stems partly from the recognition that in a context of continual change the ability to go on learning and the development of transferable skills are vital, both to our economic viability in a global economy and to the spiritual and emotional health of the country.

> To cope with rapid change and the challenge of the information age, we must ensure that people can return to learning throughout their lives. We cannot rely on a small elite, no matter how highly educated or highly paid. Instead we need the creativity, enterprise and scholarship of all our people. As well as ensuring our economic future, learning has a wider contribution. It helps make ours a civilised society, develops the spiritual side of our lives and promotes active citizenship. Learning enables people to play a full part in their community, it strengthens the family, the neighbourhood and consequently the nation.[2]

The Church

People live their lives in the world and try to relate their faith to the structures, relationships and questions they encounter. Many of them feel that their Sunday church lives do not provide the opportunity or space to support them as they grapple with these issues. It is also clear that some people prefer Sunday church to remain a haven of 'otherness' because they value a time and space where they do not have to think about the difficulties they face during the week.

In the last 30 years the role of lay people has changed. The growth of shared or collaborative ministry, the increase in the numbers involved in lay ministry, the development of adult education and training provision in dioceses, the growth of programmes like Alpha[3] and Emmaus[4] have all led to the thawing out of what Mark Gibbs described as 'God's frozen people'.[5]

Lay people's role in relation to giving has also changed. The financial pressures of the 1980s meant that the Church was no longer able to rely on its investments and historic resources to supply the needs of ordained ministry and service to the nation. Lay people have increased their financial commitment alongside their commitment of time and talents. For some this has also meant a desire to have more influence on how that money is spent. The Church needs to address the perception that more value is given to those who are accredited lay ministers and those in professional occupations, and that greater recognition is given to areas of the Church's traditional involvement, e.g. education and health.

The pattern of church attendance reflects the diversity of the society in which we live. There has been a decline in the numbers of lay people attending church every Sunday. Alongside the growth of Alpha courses and other adult learning has come a variance in the attendance pattern –

many Christians now lead such complex family and work lives that attending worship every Sunday is no longer an option.

The recently published *Youth A Part*[6] reported on the different pattern of spirituality amongst young people and reflected the difficulty some parishes have in attracting and keeping members of the younger generation. Many people of all ages are searching for a spiritual direction and orientation to the world in which they live. There seems to be little opportunity to help them to discern where God is leading them.

The Decade of Evangelism has asked lay people to reconsider their own faith and to develop skills in sharing it with those around them. The desire to do this is still hampered by considerable lack of confidence in many, though the growth of lay evangelists in some dioceses is very encouraging.

3

The Current Situation

The dioceses

In order to ascertain current provision and opportunity for learning and reflection in response to *All Are Called* and *Called to Be Adult Disciple*, the Working Group wrote to Diocesan Adult Education and Lay Training Advisers. Their responses indicate a depth of commitment to supporting and encouraging the discipleship of lay people.

Diocesan strategies

Immediately after the publication of *All Are Called* and *Called to Be Adult Disciples* there was a flurry of diocesan activity. A few dioceses appointed officers whose main task was to facilitate learning that enabled lay people to reflect on their faith and daily lives.

> *The task of working with laity in terms of making connections between faith and life and in helping lay people to reflect theologically are among the main parts of my work . . . We are tackling this task both by the range of modular courses which are available to all lay people throughout the diocese and also now through the provision, which is in development, of a Christian Foundations Course for offer to parishes.*
>
> Diocesan Adult Training Adviser, Exeter

However, through the late 1980s and early 1990s the Church of England's financial difficulties began to bite and dioceses had to look carefully at the funding of diocesan posts. A decline in the number of ordained priests was forecast and dioceses began to focus on the development of shared or collaborative ministry teams. Diocesan adult education provision moved into training people for specific lay ministries rather than educating them for lay living. In some dioceses this training continued to include reflection on the demands of daily Christian living, but in many this came second to the need for training for specific local ministries.

However, the call of all God's people has been at the heart of the theology behind many diocesan strategy documents.

EXAMPLES OF DIOCESAN STRATEGY STATEMENTS

In Oxford's Diocesan Vision and Priorities paper, Priority C has to do with the integration of faith and daily life:

> *The integration of faith and work: Our faith needs to be expressed in our work and at our work. There is a particular need to help people working in industry, finance or commerce to work out their Christian vocation in those spheres. But whether our work is at home or outside, whether it is paid or voluntary, we need to strive for greater integration.*

It moves on to offer suggestions about areas in which targets might be set, including reflecting the target in worship, through prayers, readings and sermons and through Faith and Work groups.

In Durham the bishop's preliminary strategy document (1995) made specific mention of lay witness in the world.

> *Ministry is derived from our baptism and discipleship and therefore involves the whole people of God. Most Christians who are not ordained to diaconate and priesthood exercise their ministry primarily in the secular world. Indeed it is there that the mission of the Church is seen at its sharpest and it is there that the holy, sanctifying nature of the Church infects the wider world. Surely then the preparation of the laity for this task is a top priority . . . We are looking for encouragement and training which will clarify and deepen faith, develop skills and be exercised in partnership . . . Here we would emphasise that if the church is to move into missionary mode, it needs to give honour to the witness ministry of lay people in the secular world. Their training (by secular lay people) needs careful and skilled attention which recognises both the excitement and dangers of this area of ministry . . . the Bishop will license Parish Ministry teams, including clergy as well as lay people and with a lay member in charge of Secular Ministry.*

Derby's Diocesan Strategy for Ministry policy, set out in a document called A *Better Way*, includes the theological basis for its thinking and strategic planning:

> *Ministry is the outward expression of our inner Christian faith and discipleship. All faithful disciples have a ministry. It finds expression in a whole variety of ways depending on each person's particular gifts, commitments and life situation. It is as much to do with the place*

where we work, our home and family life, the interests we pursue, the organisations to which we belong, as it is to do with the place where we worship.

For most Christians most of the time, their ministry is going to be exercised where they live and work, not in church. For too long the Church has tended to define ministry in 'churchy' terms, not in terms of the Kingdom of God. One of the greatest gifts the laity has to offer is making connections between what goes on in church and everyday life and work. The encouragement and releasing of this gift will transform the Church and our everyday ministry . . . for these profound theological reasons Synod believes that 'A Better Way' to structure the Church's ministry is to base a strategy on the ministry of all the baptised, and not just upon the clergy . . . this means that all the baptised (children, young people and adults) are called.

The report goes on to discuss ordained and lay ministry, saying: 'All that follows is in support of this fundamental ministry of the baptised.'

Diocesan programmes

Dioceses have also included lay discipleship in existing courses, such as Bishops' Certificate Courses or Foundation Courses, or they have developed specific short courses to try and address these issues at local parish level. In Chelmsford it is part of the diocesan adult education programme and part of the work of Industrial Mission (IM) chaplains working ecumenically. The Urban Learning Programme in Newham works specifically in this area. Salisbury has held residential conferences designed for people who are seeking spiritual resources for busy working lives and encourages the use of material produced by Cassell called *Sunday, Monday – Faith in the World*.[1]

Southwell Diocese held a 'God on Monday' conference in 1997 and have a page in the diocesan newspaper so that the topic is kept on the Church's agenda. They also include a very strong focus on relating life and faith in their 'Exploring Your Ministry' course which works hard to affirm people's whole life experience and God's call in the world. 'Ask yourself the question, "How am I meant to be serving God?" Whether you work for a living, whether you are retired or unemployed, you can explore new possibilities for ministry in this new course' ('Exploring Your Ministry').

Southwark includes faith, theology and action links in the course on which its pastoral auxiliaries are trained. Carlisle offers a home study course with a day school to examine the role of laity in the Church and the world, and to explore personal calling.

Oxford encourages non-stipendiary ministers and readers in secular employment to use their experience as a special focus for this concern and uses the insights of Industrial Missioners to help parishes in their thinking. Oxford also has a Diocesan Adviser in Faith and Economic Life with a key piece of their job description relating to helping the Church integrate faith and work/economic issues. A Reader Conference was entirely devoted to the ministry of readers in helping the Church to relate faith to daily life.

Bradford Diocese included Cursillo as part of their response, saying that it is very effective when used properly in helping people to transform their weekday lives in the light of their faith.

> *What is Cursillo? . . . a movement of the Church . . . helps Christians who are already committed Church members to examine where they stand in their spiritual lives and to discover how they can be used for the Lord's work in the ordinary circumstances of their lives.*[2]

In the Church in Wales the Diocese of Monmouth is looking at 'growing' churches and working with them on a number of questions including:

- Does people's Monday to Saturday reality impinge on the worship in any way?

- What sorts of activities (other than a list previously given of 'church-type' activities) are people within the Church involved with?

- How is their contribution in other activities owned by the Church?

The Mirfield Centre is part of Mirfield Theological College. Its aim is to make faith and life questions the centre of its work. It has established a women's group and hopes soon to have groups for schoolteachers and people in business. It has also developed a connection with the Institute for British Liberation Theology. There is a developing link with local dioceses and the Centre runs two days on Wakefield's Ministry Training Scheme.

Case studies
Work in three dioceses was examined more closely in order to give further insights to some of the successes and blocks when attempting to link faith and life.

LINCOLN (ADULT EDUCATION ADVISER)

Lincoln was one of the first dioceses to set up a training scheme for lay and ordained local ministry. It also has a long and clear commitment to the education of lay people so that they can live out their Christian faith in their daily lives. This responsibility comes under the job description of the Adult Education Adviser. The current adviser is a laywoman who has been in post for ten years. The first item on her job description is: 'Keeping the centrality of lay education in the minds of diocesan decision makers, drawing attention to the effects of diocesan policies and strategies and reinforcing the process of lay development'.

In 1997 a group under the chairmanship of the diocesan bishop reviewed the post and concluded:

> In addition to our recommendations we wish to give a strong affirmation of what we believe adult education is . . . We believe that all Christians are called to discipleship and service through their baptism. Growth in Christ comes through worship, learning and active service in the world. The Church and the world need an articulate and educated laity, who have an awareness of God's presence and work in the world, and who are willing to develop the skills and talents God has given them. This demands that the centrality of adult education is kept firmly in the minds of all diocesan policy makers, and that processes for lay development have a high profile in the life of the diocese. Both laity and clergy need encouragement to be committed to these principles at all levels of diocesan life.

The review confirmed the main task of the post as 'specific tasks which focus on adult education and lay people's responsibility to live out their discipleship in the world'.

The work is done in these ways:

- The main focus of the diocesan strategy for discipleship in the world is Exploring Our Faith (see below).

- The commitment to complementary ministries includes looking at the role of lay life in worship. Working with people on how to lead intercessions, and helping them to focus on the content of the intercessions, thinking about what each person is 'bringing with them' into worship, has been a useful way of moving parishes on in their understanding of the relationship between liturgy and daily life.

● Work is undertaken with individual parishes on lay education courses which always include some focus on daily discipleship.

Lincoln's diocesan structures are designed to encourage co-operation between specific areas of responsibility and this work is shared with other colleagues and the Adult Education Support Group. Lincoln is a heavily rural diocese and work on gathering people together to think about their faith and work is quite difficult. Exploring Our Faith is a Bishop's Certificate Course which uses the Bible, tradition, experience and the learner's own response to these things. It aims to help people to make a practical response to their faith either in or out of the gathered Church. It works both within and across parish boundaries. It is not about learning just for the sake of it, and rather than being church-focused it is concerned with the question 'How does this affect our lives?' Disciplined reflection is a strong theme throughout the course, and because of this it is heavily reliant on good tutors who can enable such reflection. Tutor training is a very important part of the adviser's work.

The course includes the following core areas:

● Opening the Bible.

● God in the world.

● Worship.

● Living as Christians. This final module looks specifically at lay discipleship over four sessions and a quiet day. It asks questions such as:

    – What difference does it make?

    – What are the marks of a Christian lifestyle?

    – What actually helps you: worship, Bible, Church?

It makes use of the Common Statement from *All Are Called* (see Appendix 1).

Possible options during the second year are Ways of Praying, The Old Testament, The New Testament, Exploring Doctrine, and The Church and the Churches. All of these areas of study continue the reflection on the content of learning in terms of lay life and discipleship. The course has been running since 1990 and has about 90 people in each of its two years. Those involved have included local councillors, school governors, nurses, and others involved in community action and support. It has become a seedbed for local ministry and readers, as well as being a foundation for parish growth.

The adviser's own reflections on what helps and hinders the development of this work are as follows:

What helps?

- The fact that she has been in post a long time, and is a lay person, is respected in the diocese and is seen to represent education for the whole of daily living rather than local ministry.

- She has the strong support of the diocesan bishop.

- Parish clergy are supportive.

- The open style of the material means that it can be used with people from widely differing educational backgrounds.

- The units for the course are all written over weekends in a collaborative style by a mixed lay and clerical group, and the group which writes the course is on the watch all the time for any clericalization of the material or the content.

- There are good tutors who are well trained and who can work effectively with material written by other people.

What hinders?

- Parishes which are very conservative, where people are looking for answers rather than wanting to work with experience.

- Parishes with little or no investment in developing the role of lay people.

- Bad tutoring which means that students are not encouraged or helped to make the required links between the material and their own life experience.

LIVERPOOL
(LAITY DEVELOPMENT OFFICER FOR LIFE AND WORK)

Liverpool Diocese has a long commitment to the education and training of lay people. The Laity Development Officer for Life and Work belongs to a Laity Development Team which is part of the Board of Mission and Unity. There are three officers, two full time and one dual role appointment. The aim of this particular post is to keep the issue of faith and work in front of people and this is done in a variety of ways through letters to PCCs, magazine articles, brochures and training programmes.

The work is done in the following ways:

- Spirituality courses are part of the whole team's work, and a course which had the aim of focusing on relating faith and work was initially popular, but when people began the course they found it quite difficult.

- At a recent diocesan conference for over 300 lay people the workshop which looked at life and work, the 'Spirituality of Everyday Life', was very popular.

- One course, 'Working with Faith', was jointly devised and run with Industrial Mission. The course covered five sessions (which were repeated) and included one in which people were asked to share the work they did, followed by discussion and prayer. 'A five session adult education course designed for those who wish to explore the relationship between their Christian faith and their work experience' (brochure).

- An annual conference is held with the Executive Officers of the City Council.

- 'Making Faith Work' is a four- to six-week course which gives church members an opportunity to talk about their work situation and issues that arise. 'It is important to affirm the experience of Christians in the world and to offer support and encouragement in helping them to live as Christians. To discuss how we can maintain Christian standards in a society whos e values are increasingly secular and materialistic' (brochure).

- A new diocesan course called 'A Faith to Live By' is using a new approach. 'This course is different. The course starts with your experience as a Christian in the world. It is a stimulating combination of case studies, group work, creative Bible study, teaching, scene setters, prayer and meditation, discussion and teaching. The discoveries you make on this journey will enable you to live more faithfully in a fast-moving world. This course is for people who want to take God, the Bible and the world seriously, people who are prepared to face the challenge of connecting faith, spirituality and life' (brochure).

- As part of a Mission Assessment Programme a parish audit was offered on 'what you are doing and how the Church can support you'. Six or eight parishes took this up. For the audit, the officer met the core group in a parish and assigned tasks. There was a service to launch the audit and an away day that produced an Agenda for Action. Parishes looked at what is happening now, what the community needs might be and what the priorities in the life of the Church are. This did not work very well in some Urban Priority Area (UPA) parishes because of a language and concept barrier.

- Special Harvest services in which suggestions are offered in order to include work, e.g. putting symbols of work on the altar, coming to the service in your work clothes or putting on a series of talks on work.

Some things did not really succeed:

- A parish audit on adult learning and faith and work. The whole team planned it but the area was found to be too broad, too difficult to unpack.

- Trying to get people to look at 'vocation'.

- Setting up networks or consultations with professional people. This seems to work better when the chaplains with specific responsibility for those professions take this on, and some professionals already have their own groups and do not want to meet across their own disciplines.

The officer's own reflections on the blocks and hindrances to her work in this area are these:

- The question of lay 'vocation' seems to be too challenging. There are a number of reasons why this might be so. People feel some guilt at not living up to an ideal image of what lay vocation is. The whole area seems to be too vast and it raises questions they are powerless to deal with.

- Lay people have very mixed reactions – part of them wants to discuss the issue and part does not. There is some resistance to discussing work issues in their own churches; there is a feeling that others may not understand the issues sufficiently.

- Churches have a lot of retired and unemployed people who do not want to focus too much on work; the issue of faith and life is somehow more difficult to define.

- For those who are in work, that work is often so demanding that it is hard for them to stand back and reflect on it.

- People are afraid that discussion of faith in the workplace means a particular sort of evangelism.

- It seems to work best when it is introduced to an already established group, e.g. a house group, or where it builds on previous courses such as Alpha.

- Churches are sometimes so overwhelmed by keeping the show on the road as they plug the gaps in the welfare system that they find it hard to prioritize.

- These issues are not on the agenda of the clergy.

- People find the idea of 'ordinary' lay people being involved in these areas too new and difficult a concept.

LONDON
(COMMUNITY MINISTRY)

London is a densely populated diocese with a long established area system. One diocesan-wide initiative is that of Community Ministry, which developed from an earlier Social Responsibility Department. Two advisers cover the whole diocese and divide the work by deaneries: those in which more than half the parishes are designated as UPAs and those with fewer than half UPA parishes. Both advisers have the task of supporting parishes with church-based projects, and helping parishes to develop such initiatives. There are fewer church-based community projects in the more suburban areas. In the more UPA deaneries the focus is on the church in its gathered mode and encouraging the gathered church to work on a non-church agenda. In the less UPA deaneries the Adviser is concerned with the church in its more dispersed mode, with people exercising their ministry as Christians in their daily lives.

After discussion with the two advisers we agreed to focus on the work in the less UPA deaneries. The Adviser there saw his main tasks as to affirm what is already happening; to provide a possible focus on partnership; and to work with people so that they actually recognize what they are already doing as a legitimate Community Ministry which is part of their discipleship as Christians and to be acknowledged and celebrated as part of church life.

Although encouraged and supported by the diocese through bishops and synod there is no written diocesan strategy underpinning this work. The way that the diocese is internally structured means that in some of the areas the focus on faith and life or faith and work comes under the brief of an Area Officer for Parish Development or Lay Ministry. London is also unusual in not having diocesan Industrial Missioners so that any specific work on faith and work is likely to be picked up in individual parishes – usually by the clergy.

The adviser works in a variety of ways with individual parishes or with deanery groups:

- On parish weekends where he encourages people to reflect on where God already is and how this impinges on the Church.

- Helping those people who do work in projects to think theologically – this tends to be focused on the professionals (i.e. those who are paid) rather than the volunteers.

- In deaneries, helping people to learn how to make connections between their voluntary work and their faith.

EXAMPLE

An evening for a deanery 'Celebration of Faith in Voluntary Work' was planned and put on by a group from the deanery with the Area Parish Ministry Development Adviser and the Community Ministry Adviser. The evening grew from a feeling that:

> Much of the focus of the church's involvement with the wider community in the Diocese tends to be on church based community projects, whilst less emphasis is given to the work of individual Christians 'exercising their discipleship' through their involvement as volunteers in non-church organisations or through informal networks of care such as someone helping an elderly neighbour.

> Taken from the report and review of the evening

Its aim was to:

- celebrate the diversity of voluntary work which members of the Anglican churches in . . . are already doing in their local communities;

- provide opportunities to share our experiences of being Christian in voluntary work and learn from others;

- provide opportunities to reflect on how our faith relates to our voluntary work.

About 50 people attended, representing seven out of the ten parishes in the deanery. The evening was considered to be a success. Even though many people had attended not really knowing what to expect, the discussion groups were lively and the input from two laywomen followed by a theological reflection was much appreciated.

The adviser's own reflections on the issues and questions raised by his work began with the theological question that he feels underpins how people respond to what he is trying to achieve. 'Where is God? Is God already in the world or not? Are we taking God into a godless world or revealing God already at work there?' The very different responses to this question have an enormous effect on how people are able to make links between what can be seen as secular and what is sacred. Many people tend to compartmentalize faith and Sunday and daily life, and those in leadership in churches are also struggling to make these connections.

- He had found that where there is an existing emphasis on lay involvement or lay ministry there is more encouragement for links to be made.

- He spoke of the need to demystify the language which describes the connections so that lay people can find a language which speaks of their experience and can link it to the Bible and tradition without having to use technical or overtly theological words.

- Problems occur when the theological links are not made or where the clergy are the only people working at the link. Sometimes individual volunteers in the life of the project can manage to make the links themselves, and in other places the sermon slot is used to encourage people to share their thinking and reflection.

- What has been described as 'Apt Liturgy'[3] can be an important element in helping links to be made between the work undertaken and the faith of the Church.

- Projects can drain the energy of those who are strongly involved – particularly where the experience is not brought back into the Church.

- Bishops very much set the culture – if the bishop is committed to this way of working/thinking it is more likely to happen and to take off.

Industrial Mission

Industrial Mission has, of course, always had a strong investment in helping people to relate faith and work, and some diocesan examples demonstrate co-operation between adult education and lay training and Industrial Mission. Responses from chaplains working in Industrial Mission evidenced a great variety of excellent work.

> *Members of the Industrial Mission Association are, separately and together, networking in the area of faith and work more than ever now and several teams have very well developed programmes, including the Peterborough 'People at Work' programme.*
>
> IM Chaplain, Midlands

There is also a recognition amongst many involved in Industrial Mission that the good work which is happening through their network is not having much impact on parish or diocesan commitment to this area.

> *Clergy (not all are Anglicans) still feel threatened about being involved in a ministry in which they by definition are not the experts. In the workplace issues of their congregation members, they are 'lay' and most clergy sadly cannot cope with being in that 'weak' position.*
>
> Industrial Missioner, Eastern Region

This reluctance is not restricted to clergy: for many lay people work and church life are kept in separate boxes and they resist any attempt to make connections between them.

> *Many Christians I have encountered do not, at least initially, consider that their work and their faith have a lot to say to each other. Unless they are extremely fortunate they regard their work as a regrettable necessity, and that it is in their leisure time that they really become 'themselves' and can then address questions of faith.*
>
> Non-stipendiary minister and director of textile company

Agencies

The growth of specialist agencies and networks, many within the churches, is a sign of the importance to the Church of supporting lay people in their engagement with specific issues at local, national and international levels. Such agencies are well placed to bring people with particular concerns together in an informed and reflective forum. Some lay people look to agencies to find the support they feel they need and which they cannot, or do not, find in their local church.

Christians in Public Life

Christians in Public Life (CIPL) is an ecumenical network attempting to draw together all the agencies and church centres which are working to enable connections between faith and life (for address, see Appendix 4). CIPL produces a series of excellent discussion papers and holds occasional conferences. Many of the people quoted in this report responded because of a letter sent out with the CIPL mailing. The more negative responses came from lay people who find themselves unsupported in their local churches and for whom CIPL is a lifeline that holds them, with some difficulty, within reach of the Church.

> I cannot say that what follows is anything other than a view based on my own experience. As one who, for years, felt that she left her brains at the church door on Sunday mornings I have felt deskilled and frustrated by the attitudes of clergy and some of the more traditional worshippers.
>
> University lecturer

> Status is gained within the church through holding positions of power – to keep the church organization going for its members. No empowerment is given to those who wish to work in the world outside.
>
> Methodist laywoman

Industry Churches Forum

Industry Churches Forum (previously Industrial Christian Fellowship) is another group which offers encouragement to people who wish to become involved in relating faith and work (for address, see Appendix 4). A pamphlet on running 'Laity at Work' groups says:

> We spend much of our time in activities which have no connection with the Church. We may worship in church every Sunday, and attend house groups and prayer meetings, but still the greater part of our lives is spent among people and institutions with little sense of God's presence. For many people, the greatest demand on their time and inner resources is their daily work, but they receive little help from their churches in relating the world of work on Monday to what they find in church on Sunday, and in working out what it means to be a Christian in business, industry or commerce.

The Ridley Hall Foundation

Based at Ridley Hall in Cambridge (for address, see Appendix 4), the Foundation's vision is to participate in God's mission in the business world. The Foundation does this in three ways: by trying to understand the business environment, by discerning God's purpose for business and by applying Christian values in complex working situations. It offers seminars, consultations and publications and with the Industry Churches Forum it produces a journal called *Faith in Business Quarterly*, which includes articles on ethical and faith issues.

Questionnaire responses

The work of dioceses and specialist agencies has resulted in a growth in the scope and quality of the provision for supporting lay people in their distinctive discipleship. A questionnaire to lay members of the General Synod and a small group of young adults (see Appendix 3) indicates a mixed response to this provision.

Seventy replies were received from General Synod members representing 30 dioceses. Of the respondents 38 were men and 32 women; there were none under 30, 17 were in the age range 30–50, 48 were from the range 50–65 and 5 were over 65.

Just over half of those who responded (37) felt that they were reasonably well supported in living out their faith in their daily lives and most of these found the liturgy of Sunday worship helpful, especially sermons and intercessions. They felt that the most helpful people in giving support were other members of their local congregations (mentioned by 57 out of the 70 respondents), followed by the local clergy (53 respondents).

Clearly, General Synod members have a particular role to play at deanery and diocesan levels and many found this both challenging and supportive, and commented that it was through their membership of synods that they were enabled to make connections between faith and specific issues in daily living. However, even amongst this group of lay people there was confusion about what lay discipleship in the world means. 'I found this difficult as I did not really understand where the questions were coming from. I do a lot at diocesan level, most of which my local church is pretty disinterested in.' 'I found these questions and categories not easy to understand! A very traditional incumbent-oriented style gives little lay "space".' Some people felt totally unsupported by the institutional Church in their attempts to live out their faith: 'I am sustained by friends and the "church" as an institution is hardly concerned.'

Both Synod members and the young adults who responded to the questionnaire felt more supported in family and relationship matters than in work and leisure activities. Both found that particular groups, e.g. Christian groups at school and college or Jubilee 2000, helped. Those young adults who were working wrote that they found life quite hard in their local churches. They would like to share their experiences of life and church with people of their own age, but did not find much opportunity to do so. One wrote: 'We should look for a communal approach – a sense of doing things with and for everyone else. Am I expecting too much?' Many found real support and help through deanery and diocesan events for young people.

The responses to the questionnaire demonstrate the variety of provision and different expectations amongst lay people of all ages. Diocesan provision of education and training events is seen as very helpful, particularly for those whose local church may not take this area of lay responsibility seriously.

4

Evaluation

Clearly there have been many good developments and new initiatives taken since the ecumenical publications of the 1980s. Diocesan provision has expanded and lay education and training for lay ministry have raised expectations of and for lay people. Laity are no longer thought of as 'frozen people'. There are some excellent examples of good practice from dioceses and agencies, and clearly many lay people accept and struggle with their commitment to live out their faith in their daily lives.

It can be seen from this analysis that many dioceses and agencies have the commitment to resource lay people in their baptismal discipleship at the centre of their intention and policy. However, the intention is not always fully implemented. There is a deep and profoundly disturbing gap between intention, strategy and the reality of what is actually happening in many parishes. Bishops, local clergy and laity feel that this is an important area. However, the constraints of the daily struggle to service the institution and to 'keep the show on the road' mean that those lay people who do not have time – or are not called – to take up any specific role in their local church can be seen as less committed, less useful and somehow of less value than their fellow Christians.

> In a conversation with a congregation member she apologised for not being a 'proper' Christian. When asked about what she meant, her response was – 'Well, I don't do anything in the local church. I don't really have time.' She was secretary to the local MP, ran Neighbourhood Watch for her immediate area, was a school governor, mother and wife – yet she felt that she was not serving God or the local church through any of these activities. The church at which she worshipped had somehow given her the message that she was not 'proper' because she did not have a role in the church.
>
> A Diocesan Adult Education Adviser

> *It was interesting that only last weekend I was speaking to a minister who admitted that the watershed in his ministry occurred one Sunday when in the pulpit he viewed the congregation. For the first time he saw them, not as the steward, the church secretary, the choirmaster, etc., but as John the accountant, Jill the housewife, Bill the busman, etc. It seems to me that the change in affirming people 'where they are' in their daily life begins at the local church.*
>
> CIPL member

What is required is a culture shift that, like all culture shifts, is very difficult to produce. The historic view of lay people as somehow less knowledgeable, less educated and less committed is steadily changing. Many lay people have received theological training and take up specific roles on behalf of the Church. We have had reader ministry for over a hundred years. Other lay ministries and collaborative ministries have grown exponentially in the last twenty years. Yet these seem to have emphasized the feeling that those lay people who have no specific role in the Church are in some way second-class citizens of the kingdom.

> *I believe that Affirmation is a critical element in addressing how well (or badly) the local or national church supports laity and helps them to live out their faith in their everyday lives at work, retirement, family and community activities. Some time ago the Methodist Church produced a propositional discussion document and report concerning 'the ministry of the whole people of God' in which the issue of affirming people's ministry 'where they are' was seen as critical. It is a pity that we have not followed up the point effectively.*
>
> CIPL member

We need to find ways of affirming lay people in the activities of daily living and encouraging them to act with intent, as Christians, in every area of life. Baptismal and confirmation promises are at the heart of the faith, but for many people they do not state clearly enough the full implications of being a Christian. Being a member of the Church and thence part of the Body of Christ brings with it certain responsibilities, both for the individual and for the Church. To be the people of God involves giving and doing, as well as being and receiving.

> *The Baptismal vocation . . . leads us to promise to be part of a God-centred community that lives in grace — in the relationship we have*

> with God through Jesus Christ . . . [it is] our acceptance of the Spirit's
> co-ordination of our gifts, and the Spirit provides the energy, the
> momentum, and the context to live out the promise and to extend the
> centre in whatever arenas may be offered – whether that be workplace,
> home, school or play environments. There is no recognizable limit to
> viable vocational expression so long as we remember that vocation is
> a community enterprise . . . [1]

Most adult Christians were baptized as children and their confirmation or
acceptance of the faith for themselves may be some distance in the past;
therefore, education and training are vital in bringing this recognition of
the need to live out faith intentionally into consciousness.

> Education is really the task of the whole community, and its priorities
> are threefold for the ministering and missionary community: (1) to
> know the story, the biblical witness; (2) to know what the story
> means, the theology that gives the story momentum and the history
> that details its context and impact; and (3) to know how to live
> the story, in terms of liturgy, history and future, evangelism and
> mission, as part of the Spirit-co-ordinated community. [2]

Many of the diocesan ventures described above are attempting to take
seriously those three areas chosen by Stewart Zabriskie, the Bishop of
Nevada. At this point in history the world and the Church need lay people
who can articulate the faith they hold with confidence and live it out with
intention, challenging and showing by example of life that Christianity has
something to offer which is both unique and necessary.

Many lay people are unable to or do not want to make the connections
between faith and life. There are many reasons for this – some to do with the
pain and difficulty of working and living in cultures that challenge or ignore
deeply held belief and values. Some work done under the auspices of the
William Temple Foundation with lay people working in health and education
found that for many the need to make difficult day-to-day decisions which
were in conflict with belief was just too painful. Therefore faith was an
escape from those pressures and had to be kept in a separate compart-
ment. [3]

John Hull, in his seminal work *What Prevents Christian Adults from Learning*,
speaks of modernity bringing individualism, which in its turn produces
inner fragmentation. Each individual sees their life as a mixture of several

different roles: employee, father or mother, son or daughter, hobbies enthusiast, political activist or churchgoer.

> [T]he distinctive thing about modernity is that the segments of life and society within which each role is acted out have become largely isolated. So it is that in one's place of work, one mixes with people who are quite different from the people in one's neighbourhood, and these again may be quite different from the group with whom one shares a sporting or political involvement. Each of these is a world, having its own rules, its own pecking order and its own morality . . . [4]

He goes on to speak of a sharpened individual reality which is seen against this variety of life worlds that often have a hierarchy of meaning, so that some feel most themselves at work, others at home, others in leisure activities.

> The world of religion and church tends to become but one of these worlds, and to be placed on a similar footing to the others, in that every world is not only a role which I act, but a source of meaning for my life.[5]

His view is that these various worlds can be so separate for people that they often make little attempt to connect them.

> It is possible for a person without being hypocritical or self-consciously inconsistent to act in very different ways and on very different belief assumptions as he [sic] moves from world to world.[6]

Hull's question of how Christian adults can be educated so that their faith becomes a trans-world reality is clearly at the root of our enquiry. Whilst there is evidence that progress is being made, the culture change is slow.

5

Fruit of the Cross

In this chapter we want to set out our understanding of what it is to be lay disciples both in the Church and in the world. We call this chapter 'Fruit of the Cross' because as lay disciples we have been called to new life through Christ's redemptive sacrifice. It follows, therefore, that what we are trying to clarify is what it is to live in the world in the light of Jesus' death and resurrection.

We say 'clarify', but by this we do not mean that we are using theoretical language to answer or solve questions or problems which have arisen in previous chapters. Rather we are now concerned with the resonances that have sounded throughout the materials we have examined, and the continuities of faith and experience to which they witness. The point of this chapter, then, is not to add anything to what we have said previously, but rather to make explicit what has been implicit in the stories told by various lay disciples. In this way, we hope to explain the theological and ecclesiological bases of our understanding of lay discipleship, as they arise naturally from the material we have analysed. Out of this will come our suggested strategies for the future support and empowerment of lay disciples, and the themes of our covenant.

St Paul wrote that Christians are a new creation in Christ (2 Corinthians 5.17). Our being Christian is therefore determined by God's will as it is revealed in the life, death and resurrection of Jesus Christ: we are fruit of the cross, so to speak. Christians celebrate this reality in Holy Communion, when we witness to our participation in the Body of Christ by partaking of the bread and wine. There are various emphases at this point, but one of the most important is that we are one Body, just as there is one God. This is the Church's sacramental reality, which it celebrates in all aspects of its life.

Christians enter this one Body by dying and rising in Christ, in the power of the Holy Spirit. Baptism, consequently, is the first principle of being a Christian: we enter the new creation as we enter the Body of Christ, for they are the same. That this is true is revealed by Pentecost: Christ sends the Holy Spirit so that we might know the gospel, and that knowing we might have eternal life. Thus, there is a continuity from the Father to the Son to the Spirit, and hence to us. When we speak of grace, this is what we mean: the presence of God which sustains the Church, not just in its past and present but also in its future. We participate in this gift in faith, hope and love.

The fact that we are all Christians because we are all baptized means that we are all one Body, one People, one Church. Equality is therefore a guiding principle of the faith: one cannot be 'more' baptized than others. The significance of equality is thus not as a civil right, but rather as a characteristic of the love of God as it is revealed in Jesus Christ. When we speak of equality before God, consequently, we are making a christological point: we are baptized equally in the grace of salvation.

The laity have certain responsibilities and duties, given to them by God as revealed by Jesus Christ. The focus of lay life is in the world. It is in the ordinary conditions of daily life in which lay people find themselves that the duties of faith, hope, love and charity are expressed. It is primarily in streets and neighbourhoods, at work, in the school playground and supermarket that lay people respond to their vocation as Christians as well as in church. Together these things make up the life of discipleship in Christ, and they are undertaken in the name of Christ and the kingdom. God has given the means by which such life is sustained, primarily through the gift of the Holy Spirit, but also and importantly through the gifts of word and sacraments. Qualitatively, we do not differentiate between these gifts: just as they are equally God's, so they are equally graceful. All Christians share equally in them; that is why God gave them to us. From what we have seen in our work for this report we affirm this principle as a basis for the empowerment of lay discipleship in the contemporary world.

Over the years lay ministries, e.g. those of readers and pastoral assistants, have been recognized by the Church as means by which some of the responsibilities and duties of lay people can be realized. While it is correct and important to recognize that the Church believes that God gives deacons, priests and bishops as a sign of grace, this should not be used as an argument to marginalize either specific lay ministers or those whose focus of ministry is as disciples in the world. It is true that a large part of the people's work involves the leadership of the threefold order, be it in mission or worship, and it is right and proper for an historic institution to recognize such continuities within its own traditions. At the same time, however, the modern world is made up of an incredible diversity of societies, and the people of God is itself incredibly diverse. Just as we should celebrate that diversity for the joy and grace it brings to the Church, so we should recognize and endorse the diversity of non-clerical ministries that are found among the people, provided they truthfully reflect God's glory. Insofar as such ministries are truthfully undertaken, they are recognized by the Church as doing God's will and are therefore honoured as part of the work of the people.

It is very important to recognize diversity within the people for one very simple reason: it is intrinsically recognition of the presence of the Holy Spirit. Though it is true, therefore, that as Christians we become a new creation in Christ, as Christians we remain living in the midst of the old creation; though baptized, we remain in the midst of the unbaptized. The Church is in the world, participating in the redemption of creation, in the power of the Spirit. And it simply *is* the case that this takes place in a wide diversity of different ways. Though one, the Church is not homogenized; though one, neither is the world. To recognize that the Spirit empowers us to embrace the world in many different ways, for the sake of Jesus Christ, is to recognize grace, the presence of God. God loves us as we really are, and we really are diverse. To negate this diversity and to seek uniformity for its own sake, still more to impose it, is to compromise this expression of God's love

The experience of many of the lay people in this report shows that making a material distinction between the Church and the world does not ring true; the two are intimately related, because the Church is always in the world. New creation is not about leaving the old creation behind, but rather its redemption. The people of God witness to this in many different ways, and in so doing they are doing God's will. It follows, therefore, that one of the principal strategies for lay development is to educate the people in their responsibilities to and for the world. And as a major part of that education they should realize that they are not called to be separate from the world, but rather to be one with it.

Of course, this education and realization will involve a variety of different qualities, for example, cultural and political awareness, and responsibility for social and economic justice. In such respects, it is true that deacons, priests and bishops can and should exercise leadership, because along with diversity it is also necessary to recognize continuity, and this cannot always be achieved 'from the bottom up'. Theologically, however, we must affirm that such a practical distinction between the responsibilities of the threefold order, and those of the people as a whole, does not amount to separation. Theologically, we must speak of the people and their covenant relationship with God, as Jesus Christ reveals it. The hope of the world lies in the integration of that relationship with that revelation.

6

Strategies for Action

If the diversity of experience and expression of discipleship is a gift of God for the benefit of the Church and the world, then strategies for action to enable more lay people to act with intention on their faith cannot be constrained or restricted to one model.

This report advocates that Christians are called to live out in God's world the holiness that they derive from their baptism into Christ. Their response to the call to go out and bear fruit is not merely a priority but is essential to the mission of the Church. The communion of the Church can and should give them the encouragement and support necessary for their vocation, which is of fundamental importance to the life of the Church and for the service that the Church renders to humanity. Many examples of good practice are described in Chapter 3: diocesan initiatives will continue to be developed and lay people are creating their own networks of support or using agencies to help them in their struggle to make sense of faith and life.

However, this activity will nowhere reach its full potential and in some places may happen only at an inadequate level unless individual dioceses and parishes deliberately and definitely plan for its development. Some dioceses and parishes have undertaken such planning and their experience can be an encouragement and example. We are mindful of the caveat from the experience of the Diocese of Liverpool when an attempt was made to introduce a parish audit on adult learning, faith and work (see page 28). However, such planning is especially necessary at the parish level because it is here that the majority of church members will receive their major encouragement to mission and the indispensable support for it. The suggestions that follow are specifically directed towards parish development, but dioceses are not exempt from the planning process. They have a vital role to play in stimulating and assisting parishes in their planning by providing a strategic framework and support services that enable individual parishes to recognize possibilities and realize their capabilities. Parish and diocese need to construct a collaborative approach that will include rigorous evaluation in due course.

A process of planning for parish development

The suggestions that follow are derived from the five-stage cycle that the Standards and Effectiveness Unit of the Department for Education and Employment suggests as an effective model for school improvement.[1] Adaptation of this model makes it suitable for developing a variety of programmes for diocesan and parish development – especially in the field of education. Its other main advantage in this context is that it will already be familiar in theory and in practice to many in the Church who have roles as teachers, administrators and governors in Church or State schools.

The process of planning for parish development in the encouragement, affirmation and support of lay disciples requires not only the adoption of an adequate model, but also the adoption of appropriate ways of applying it. No model will secure development unless open and honest discussions about the parish's performance and ways of improving it are encouraged. The parish's potential for development will be inadequate unless the practical measures for improvement are developed within a strategic context and involvement and co-operation are maximized.

The five stages

STAGE 1: HOW WELL ARE WE DOING?

Looking critically at what the Church is doing in encouraging, affirming and supporting lay discipleship is the essential first step. Questions might include:

1. How many church members are engaged in voluntary service directed towards:

   - persons as individuals
   - the local community
   - the wider society
   - the developing world?

   How effective is the church's encouragement, affirmation and support of this work?

2. In what ways are we as a church engaged in voluntary service directed towards:

   - persons as individuals
   - the local community

- the wider society
- the developing world?

How effective is this voluntary service?

3. How does the church support its members in the living out of their faith as:

    - members of families
    - members of the local community
    - employees, employers, unemployed or retired

    a) through the liturgy

    b) in other ways?

    How effective is the church's encouragement, affirmation and support in these areas?

STAGE 2: HOW WELL COULD WE BE DOING?

By measuring and benchmarking its activities and achievements in encouraging, affirming and supporting lay discipleship against the claims of the gospel, the Law and the prophets, the church is better placed to judge its own performance. Questions might include:

1. In what ways can the church improve the efficiency and the effectiveness of its encouragement, affirmation and support of church members in:

    - the voluntary service they perform
    - the living out of their faith?

2. In what ways can the church improve the efficiency, effectiveness and scope of the voluntary service that we engage in as a church?

3. To what extent do we encourage or allow service in the Church to displace service in the world?

4. To what extent do we encourage or sanction the separation of the life that is actually lived from the faith that is professed, resulting in a gap between creed and deed?

5. How do parishes similar to ours, in the deanery, diocese and other dioceses, encourage and support lay discipleship in their members?

STAGE 3: WHAT MORE CAN WE AIM TO ACHIEVE IN THE NEXT TWO OR THREE YEARS?

With the information provided by Stages 1 and 2 the parish should be able to set realistic and challenging objectives. Questions might include:

1. What persons or groups are there to whom we should show more neighbourly love

    ● as individual church members

    ● as a church?

2. What more is there at the personal, community, societal and international levels that we could be doing as individual church members and as a church to help

    ● reduce poverty and inequalities

    ● promote better use and development of God's creation

    ● secure justice and human rights for those denied them

    ● seek and maintain peace and reconciliation?

STAGE 4: WHAT MUST WE DO TO MAKE IT HAPPEN?

Once the parish has set its objectives it needs to take determined action to achieve them. Questions might include:

1. What will be done?

2. At whom will it be aimed?

3. Who will be responsible for ensuring that it is done?

4. What resources and support will be helpful and necessary to ensure that it is done?

5. What will the timetable be?

STAGE 5: MAKING IT HAPPEN

The application of the earlier stages will have produced a plan for the development of lay discipleship among individual church members and in the church as a corporate body. This final stage of the cycle is necessary to ensure that the plans are implemented and modified where they do not efficiently and effectively achieve the desired results. Questions might include:

1. Are we achieving our identified objectives?

2. Are the identified resources appropriate and have they been delivered?

3. Are we keeping to our estimated time scales and, if not, how should they be amended?

4. If we are doing better than expected, to what can this be attributed, and should we raise our sights in the future?

5. If our objectives are not being fully met, what must we do to make the objectives more realistic and/or more achievable?

This process, which will need to be adapted to suit the needs of specific parishes, should offer an opportunity to create a strategic plan for each local church.

Covenant

As the conclusion to the report we offer an outline covenant between lay disciples and the Church. The aim of this covenant is to put simply what is required of lay disciples and what is required of the Church in order to empower lay people as they answer the call to new life, in a new millennium, living as God's people in the world. All Christian people are called by their baptism to: *Membership of the Church, the Body of Christ – and to being part of a process of ongoing commitment through repentance and acceptance of the love and forgiveness of God.*

> Almighty God, whose Holy Spirit equips the Church with a rich variety of gifts; grant that we may use them to bear witness to Christ by lives built on faith and love. Make us ready to live his Gospel and eager to do his will, that we may share with all your Church in the joys of eternal life . . .
>
> Eternal God, you have declared in Christ the completion of your purpose of love. May we live by faith, walk in hope and be renewed in love, until the world reflects your glory, and you are all in all. Even so; come, Lord Jesus.

The Alternative Service Book 1980

This call requires of all people 'to do justly, love mercy and walk humbly with our God'. In order to fulfil that calling all Christian people are required to:

- develop a spirituality and pattern of prayer which is consonant with their role as part of the Church in the world;

- learn so that they have a firm grounding and understanding of their faith;

- learn how to interpret and relate their faith and life experiences in order to be able to think theologically about their own context locally and globally;

- understand their role in worship and particularly in the celebration of the Eucharist;

- understand what service, mission and ministry mean for them in their particular calling and act on that understanding;

- recognize their specific calling to be God's representative in the situations in which they are placed;

- be aware of the need for continuing learning and development throughout the whole of their lives.

This requires that the whole Church:

- recognizes the importance of each person's call in the context of the Church gathered or dispersed;

- expects that each person will take their individual call seriously and will be resourced and supported in order to fulfil that calling;

- plans and takes steps to secure provision for the lifelong learning needs of all its people in their discipleship;

- develops liturgy which recognizes and celebrates the importance of the daily experience of all those worshipping together;

- values the diversity of spiritualities which enable the people of God to be faithful to the gospel.

Individual lay people and local churches can use this covenant as a way of checking how their lay discipleship is being enabled and supported.

Appendix 1

Extract from the Common Statement in *All Are Called* (1985)

Because all human beings are made in the image of God, they are called to become the people of God, the Church, servants and ministers and citizens of the Kingdom, a new humanity in Jesus Christ. Though we are tainted by our sinfulness, God's wonderful grace and love offer us all this common Christian vocation. God leaves everyone free to refuse this call; but the call is there for all without exception.

The young are called; the elderly are called. There is no retirement for the Christian pilgrimage. The beautiful are called, and also the unlovely. The sick are called as well as the healthy and the energetic. Activists are called and also quiet people. We are all called regardless of our intellectual abilities or our formal education. We are called regardless of our race or nationality or social class . . . and for everybody, bishops, priests and laity together, the great sacrament of our common calling is our baptism, which signifies our glorious new life in Christ . . . What is more, this call comes to us all, for all of our days and years and for all of our activities.

Appendix 2

Summary of Recommendations
from *Called to Be Adult Disciples* (GS 794)

We recommend that:

- each parish find ways of affirming lay vocation in its liturgy;

- the Liturgical Commission produce material that values and celebrates the daily lives and experience of lay people;

- the Board of Education support and encourage the further development and publication of work being done in the area of adult Christian learning;

- the Board of Mission and Unity undertake research into patterns of spirituality appropriate to lay vocation and look at ways in which such patterns can be developed and disseminated;

- the Advisory Council for the Church's Ministry co-operate further with the Board of Education in the areas of educational principles and practice with reference to theological education;

- each bishop appoint a senior member of staff, with clearly indicated terms of reference, to share with him the responsibility to focus and develop the role of the laity in the dispersed Church;

- the Faith and Order Advisory Group be encouraged to work further on the theology of the Church and the relationship between ordained and lay;

- all boards and councils of the General Synod (and their working parties) should work towards having a significant proportion of lay people serving on them.

Appendix 3

Questionnaire to Lay Members of General Synod and Young People

WORKING GROUP ON LAY DISCIPLESHIP

Through this questionnaire the Working Group is seeking to discover how you are supported by the Church as you practise your faith through the whole of your life. Please tick the appropriate boxes.

1. **In which of the following areas do you participate as a lay disciple?**

    In:

    your personal lifestyle choices and commitments,
    e.g. as a consumer, investor, viewer ☐

    the family to which you belong ☐

    the neighbourhood or community of which you are a
    member ☐

    the functional communities of which you are a member

    – at work ☐

    – in your leisure activities ☐

    – in voluntary work ☐

    – other (please specify) . . . . ☐

    any other groups in which you are involved, e.g. development issues, campaigning, environmental matters.

2. Does the church you attend deliberately support and help you in this lay discipleship?

In:

	Not at all	A little	Adequately	Very well
Your personal lifestyle choices and commitments	1	2	3	4
The family to which you belong	1	2	3	4
The neighbourhood or community of which you are a part	1	2	3	4
The functional communities of which you are a member				
– at work	1	2	3	4
– in your leisure activities	1	2	3	4
– in voluntary work	1	2	3	4
– other (as above)	1	2	3	4
Any other groups in which you are involved	1	2	3	4

3. How does the church do this?

a. Locally

Sunday liturgy ☐

sermon ☐

intercession ☐

groups during the week ☐

special events ☐

other (please specify) ....

b.   Deanery   ☐

Please specify in what ways ....

....

c.   Diocese   ☐

Please specify in what way ....

....

d.   Any other agencies, groups or networks   ☐

Please specify what they are. ....

....

4.   Who in your church helps you in your lay discipleship?

other members of the congregation   ☐

lay ministers/leaders   ☐

reader(s)   ☐

clergy   ☐

the PCC   ☐

5.   In which areas would you like more help as a lay disciple?

In:

your personal lifestyle choices and commitments   ☐

the family to which you belong   ☐

the neighbourhood or community of which you
are a part   ☐

the functional communities of which you are a
member   ☐

–   at work   ☐

–   in your leisure activities   ☐

–   in voluntary work   ☐

–   other (as overleaf)   ☐

other groups in which you are involved (as overleaf).

6.   **In the church you attend how much are you able to share your experience of being a lay disciple?**

In:

	Not at all	A little	Adequately	Very well
Your personal lifestyle choices and commitments	1	2	3	4
The family to which you belong	1	2	3	4
The neighbourhood or community of which you are a part	1	2	3	4
The functional communities of which you are a member				
At work	1	2	3	4
In your leisure activities	1	2	3	4
In voluntary work	1	2	3	4
Other (as above)	1	2	3	4
Any other groups in which you are involved	1	2	3	4

Diocese: ....   M ☐   F ☐

Age: Under 30 ☐   30–50 ☐   50–65 ☐   over 65 ☐

Is your main activity: Paid employment ☐ Voluntary work ☐ Running a home ☐

Other (please specify)...

Church setting: Mainly urban ☐   Mainly rural ☐

Appendix 4
Useful Publications, Addresses and Contacts

Publications

David Bosch, *Transforming Mission – Paradigm Shifts in the Theology of Mission*, Orbis Books, 1991.

Bernard Braley and Richard Michelmore, *Touching the Pulse – Worship and Where We Work*, Stainer and Bell, 1996.

Cameron Butland, *Work in Worship*, Hodder and Stoughton, 1985.

David Clark, *Changing World; Unchanging Church? An Agenda for Christians in Public Life*, Mowbray, an imprint of Cassell Publishers, 1997.

Faith in Business Quarterly, the journal of the Ridley Hall Foundation and the Industry Churches Forum.

Edmund Flood and Jack Dominian, *The Everyday God, Changing Lives at Home and at Work*, Geoffrey Chapman, 1993.

Leslie Francis and Philip Richer, *Gone but not Forgotten*, Darton, Longman and Todd, 1998.

Rowland Goodwin, *Living in the Fast Lane – Mission Alongside the Powerful and Influential*, Methodist Publishing House, 1991.

Celia Allison Hahn, 'Empowering the saints through shared ministry', *Action Information*, May/June 1987.

Richard Higginson, *Called to Account: Adding Value in God's World*, Eagle and Highland, 1993.

Richard Higginson, *Transforming Leadership: A Christian Approach to Management*, SPCK, 1996.

Christifideles Laici (The Lay Faithful), Holy See, 30 January 1989.
Available from the Catholic Truth Society.

Frank McHugh, Malcolm Pitt and Malcolm Grundy, *Layers of Creativity – A Christian Response to the World of Work*, The Vicarage, Gisburn, Clitheroe, Lancs. BB7 4HR, 1994.
A new look at the papal encyclicals with regard to the world of work.

Ann Morisy, *Beyond the Good Samaritan*, Mowbray, an imprint of Cassell Publishers, 1997.

Richard Niebuhr, *Christ and Culture*, Faber and Faber, 1952.

Stewart Zabriskie, *Total Ministry*, Alban Institute, 1995.

Courses

Sunday, Monday – Faith in the World, Cassell, 1995.
A six-session ecumenical course for groups to look at how to carry their Sunday faith into their lives on Monday and through the week.

Graham Dow, *A Christian Understanding of Daily Work*, Grove Books.
A study course.

Richard Higginson, *Mind the Gap: Connecting Faith with Work*, Ridley Hall Foundation.
A workbook – why do so many local churches take little or no interest in the work that their congregations do?

A New Way of Being Church.
Programme offered in course format by the United Society for the Propagation of the Gospel, Partnership House, 157 Waterloo Road, London SE1 8XA.

People and Work – A Personal Ministry Course for Lay People.
Lay Training Opportunities, Peterborough House, 90 Harleston Road, Northampton NN5 7AG.

Unemployment and the Future of Work, enquiry compiled by Anton Baumohl.
A workbook, Council of Churches for Britain and Ireland, Inter-Church House, 35–41 Lower Marsh, London SE1 7RL.

Useful contacts

British Anglican Cursillo Council, President: David Lawson, 3 Devon Circus, Redhill, Nottingham NG5 8JG.

Christians in Public Life (CIPL), Westhill College, Selly Oak, Birmingham B29 6LL. Also contact The Human City Initiative and for more information see *Christian Agencies – Who's Who?* (CIPL).

Christians in Secular Ministry (CHRISM), contact Revd Phil Aspinall, Industrial Mission, Diocese of Coventry.

Industrial Mission Association, Moderator: Revd Canon Denis Claringbull, 17 Merrivale Crescent, Ross on Wye HR9 5JU.

Industry Churches Forum, 86 Leadenhall St, London EC3A 3DH.

The Institute for Contemporary Christianity, St Peter's, Vere St, London W1M 9HP.

The Methodist Church's 'Vocations Sunday', Methodist Church House, Marylebone Rd, London.

Methodists in Industry, Business and Commerce (MIBIC), contact the Revd Harold Clarke, 130A Southdown Road, Harpenden, Herts AL5 1PU.

Managerial and Organisational Disciples for the Enhancement of Ministry (MODEM), Suite 503, Premier House, 10 Greycoat Place, London SW1P 1SB.

The Ridley Hall Foundation, Ridley Hall, Cambridge CB3 9HG.

The William Temple Foundation, Manchester Business School, Manchester M15 6PB.

Notes

Introduction

1. Board of Education of the General Synod, *All Are Called*, CIO Publishing, 1985.
2. Board of Education of the General Synod, *Called to Be Adult Disciples*, Board of Education, 1987.
3. *Christifideles Laici* (The Lay Faithful), Holy See, 30 January 1989. Available from the Catholic Truth Society.
4. *The Ministry of the Whole People of God*, Methodist Publishing House, 1988.

Chapter 2: The context

1. CCBI, *Unemployment and the Future of Work*, see Appendix 4.
2. David Blunkett, Secretary of State for Education and Employment, in the Foreword to *The Learning Age, a Renaissance for a New Britain*, Department for Education and Employment, 1998.
3. Alpha Courses, HTB Publications, Holy Trinity, Brompton Road, London SW7 1JA.
4. Emmaus Courses, Bible Society/National Society/Church House Publishing, 1996.
5. Mark Gibbs, *God's Frozen People*, Collins, 1964. A book for and about ordinary Christians.
6. Board of Education of the General Synod, *Youth A Part*, Church House Publishing, 1996.

Chapter 3: The current situation

1. *Sunday, Monday – Faith in the World*, Cassell, 1995.
2. Taken from a leaflet produced by the British Anglican Cursillo Council.
3. Ann Morisy, *Beyond the Good Samaritan*, Mowbray, 1997.

Chapter 4: Evaluation

1. Stewart Zabriskie, *Total Ministry*, Alban Institute, 1995, p. 9.
2. Ibid., p. 19.
3. Rachel Jenkins, *Changing Times, Unchanging Values*, William Temple Foundation, 1991.
4. John Hull, *What Prevents Christian Adults from Learning*, SCM, 1985.
5. Ibid., p. 28.
6. Ibid.

Chapter 6: Strategies for action

1. Setting Targets for Pupil Achievement – Guidance for Governors, DfEE Standards and Effectiveness Unit, 1997. From *Targets to Action – Guidance to Support Effective Target Setting for Schools*, DfEE Standards and Effectiveness Unit, 1997.

Index